Growth Hacking

———— ✎✎✎✎ ————

The Best Kept Marketing Secrets Of
Startup Hackers And Entrepreneurs

By Logan King

Table of Contents

Introduction

It's challenging to manage a business these days, much less grow it. It's because unlike generations ago, it's much easier to get into business now, especially with the advent of the Internet age that pretty much leveled the business field.

As such, the level of competition is so much higher than in generations past and you'll need to constantly up your game if you want your business to experience great growth and survive today's competitive business environment.

In this book, you'll learn what it takes to hack your business' way to significant growth as fast as possible, specifically by harnessing the power of that single biggest force that has changed the way business is done forever – the Internet.

You'll discover that single biggest secret to growing your business and the practical ways you can implement or apply that secret using the Internet. You'll also read a couple of successful growth hacking stories from 2 of the most successful startups in the world today – Uber and Snapchat – to get an idea of how the secret works.

By the end of this book, you'll be in a great position to start taking steps towards hacking your business' growth.

If you're ready, turn the page and let's begin!

Chapter 1:

The Single-Minded Secret
To Growing Your Website
Or Business

"I think one of the bigger lessons the Internet has taught us is that 'niche' or 'subculture' are a lot bigger than anyone ever thought." – Warren Ellis

I have a confession to make. After all these years, I'm still in awe of the magnifying glass. Not only does it help me see small things in great detail, it also gives ordinary light the power to burn through paper and other materials. In fact, you may think of a laser as light passing through a super-duper power magnifying glass, which allows it to burn or cut through just about anything.

What's the secret to the magnifying glass's ability to turn ordinary light into a weapon of destruction – or construction, depending on the intentions? One word: focus. By concentrating all of the energy of light into just one small spot on a surface, a magnifying glass makes ordinary light extremely powerful.

Chapter 1: The Single-Minded Secret To Growing Your Website Or Business

When it comes to many things in life that don't involve burning, focus is just as important and powerful when it comes to achieving great results. In most cases, the single biggest difference between a great product or business and mediocre or even failing ones is the ability to zero in and focus.

Generations ago, it's standard practice for businesses to brand themselves as convenience stores would – one stop shops where everything and anything you may need is available in just one location. It's the same concept for department stores where you can find a huge variety of items in just one visit.

Now there's nothing wrong with that, especially when you're talking about practicality. But if you're looking for the best quality products, those are often found not in general stores but in specialized or boutique ones.

Because of the advent of the Internet age, which makes it possible for many smaller suppliers to sell specialized or boutique products online with minimal to no cost at all, the advantages associated with general stores are starting to dwindle, if it hasn't already. For one, customers no longer need to get out of the house on a very hot summer day or on a day when it's raining cat's and dogs just to buy something they like.

Second, the proliferation of so many small and independent suppliers makes it possible to find special items that you are looking for in particular. And third, the reason why small suppliers are able to thrive in the Internet age is because their markets are no longer limited to the immediate geographical area where they're located – the whole world has practically become their market. W

Take for example a personal finance consultation service. Even if the city you live in are full of people who are already well off or financially literate, you can expand your service's market to areas outside your city – the whole country even.

Why? It's because you can offer consultancy services online and therefore, people who may live on the other end of your country can avail of your consultancy services via a videoconference via Skype or Viber. You're no longer limited to your physical area.

Or how about conducting investment management seminars to an audience who lives in different countries? How can you conduct such seminars for people living in Japan, Norway, the Philippines, or Saudi Arabia without having to go to those countries or having your participants fly over to where you are?

Again, via the Internet through what's called a Webinar, or a seminar done over the Web. So if you're starting a business or already have an existing one that you'd like to grow by leaps and bounds, then you'll need to focus your efforts just like a magnifying glass does to light.

But the question is: where do you focus your efforts?

Niche Markets

Simply put, a niche market is a focused market. For example, the automotive industry is a very big – and general – market.

While you may consider people who want or need to buy cars as a specific market within the general automotive market, as compared to people who are looking to buy accessories for their cars, you can break that market down further into something highly focused, such as those who are sports car enthusiasts, environmental crusader types of drivers like Leonardo DiCaprio who chooses to drive an environment friendly car like a Prius over fancier gas-guzzling cars, or those who want big cars capable of running on both paved and off roads.

So why is focusing on a niche market very important for growth hacking your business? There are a couple of reasons for this. First is being on top of prospects' minds. When you focus your business on a specific niche, people will most probably view you as an expert in that particular field or niche.

What that means is when they want to purchase products or services related to yours, they'd come to you first rather than the generic stores or service providers in the market.

Speaking of being an expert, focusing your business on a niche market will also give you're the opportunity to become an even better expert in the field of business you're in. It's because if you're focused, you don't have to burden yourself with knowing as much as you can about as much topics and current developments normally associated with general market businesses.

You avoid spreading yourself too thinly and are able to focus your time and efforts on a few important areas, which will allow you to learn those things much more deeply.

And the more of an expert you become, the more your stock as an expert in your field rises, which is in and by itself already a great promotional advantage for growing your business.

Another growth hack advantage to focusing on a market niche, which is a result of the first advantage, is people will most likely agree to patronize your products or services even at a premium.

Why? It's because if they see you as an expert in that field, they'll feel more secure transacting with you and with such value on trust and quality these days, they'll more likely be willing to pay extra bucks. Just take a look at the iPhone, the price of its cheapest model alone is equivalent to about 10 units of other cheap competitors. Despite its high price tag, many people still patronize it. Why? Because of the quality and trust in the brand.

The third reason for focusing on a market niche is the result of the second one: higher profits. The more profitable your business is, the more you can afford to make your products and services even better, work less, and enjoy life more! It then becomes a self-sustaining spiral of joy and productivity.

And profitability can even be enhanced through lower costs as you'll have to carry a wide range of stocks of various products, many of which may not sell well and get you stuck with slow moving inventory, that most other general businesses are stuck with.

Lastly, a business cannot afford to neglect its presence on the Internet if it wants to experience significant growth in this day and age. The same goes for your business or website. Being focused on a particular niche, the more concentrated information on your businesses web site or social media page becomes.

Chapter 1: The Single-Minded Secret To Growing Your Website Or Business

High concentration of related information is one important factor for ranking well in search engine results of major search engines like Google, Yahoo and Bing. And the more people see you on line, the more potential customers you have.

More Is Less And Less Is More?

One of the concerns about being too specific, i.e., focusing on a particular market niche, is that the potential customer base is much less than compared to a general business. That's actually true – a niche-focused business has a smaller market than a generalized one. After all, a niche market is but a subset of a general or bigger one.

But it's not just about the market size – it's also about the quality. Take for example luxury cars like BMW. They definitely have a smaller market compared to, say, Toyota, whose market is made up of just about everybody who can afford to buy and drive a car – from ordinary middle-class employees to big businessmen.

But why does BMW continue to do well as a business despite the "smaller" market share?

It's because it's focused on serving the relatively few people who have relatively huge amounts of money to spare for the grander things in life. In other words, they have targeted a market that may be small in number but huge in bank accounts. Such is the power of focusing on the right market niche.

Another aspect to quality of prospects or market is the probability of people actually patronizing your business. Generally speaking, if you get into a business that focuses on a rather big market that's already relatively saturated with many competitors, the chances of people actually availing of your products and services may be very low compared to putting up a business that's geared towards a specific market niche where competitors are far and few in between or even non-existent.

In other words, focusing your business on a big and general market that's saturated with competitors makes your business a small fish in a big pond while focusing on a niche market can make your business a big fish in a small pond.

Growth Hack Success Story: Uber

One of the best success stories about growth hacking via niche marketing is Uber. I'm sure you've already heard about this company that offers ride-sharing services, which was founded by Garret Camp and Travis Kalanick in 2009. The two founded what was then a startup company to address a particular market niche – disgruntled cab riders.

During that time, San Francisco City was experiencing serious issues with the taxi service industry and the duo decided to do something about it – put up Uber and develop the app.

At first, the app and the service was launched in their native city of San Francisco. Because it was able to successfully meet the needs of the San Francisco niche market of disgruntled cab riders, it was able to expand operations to New York the following year, which still focused on the same niche market, which has grown to include disgruntled riders of other public forms of transportation.

Again, its ability to focus on the right market niche – disgruntled public transport riders – and successfully meets their needs and expectations allowed Uber to experience phenomenal growth, which has taken its operations all over the world from its humble beginnings in San Francisco. Just how big has the company grown? Think $10 billion in annual revenue.

Yes, that's a "b" and not an "m" in front of the word "illion".

So how did Uber serve its niche market en route to phenomenal growth? First, it focused on filling in the serious gaps that most traditional taxi companies weren't able to – convenience. Unlike traditional cab companies, Uber allows you to get a ride from just about anywhere there's an Uber-registered vehicle nearby using your smart phone.

You don't have to walk for several blocks praying to God that an empty cab with a trustworthy driver comes along in the middle of the night.

Uber also provides much better customer service compared to most traditional taxi companies, as most Uber drivers are driven by owners of the vehicles themselves and Uber has an excellent system of tracking, monitoring and evaluating their registered vehicles, and their drivers or owners. With such accountability in place, the risks for hailing a cab driven by a mad man is very, very low.

No wonder Uber's growth hacking story has been nothing short of phenomenal. By identifying a great market niche, that of disgruntled commuters, they were able to put up a startup business that has grown by leaps and bounds in less than 10 years. Such is the power of the niche markets for start up businesses.

<u>Growth Hack Success Story: Snapchat</u>

Another great example of successfully focusing on a niche market for phenomenal growth is Snapchat. It's basically a mobile application program that lets you shoot pictures and vides with short life spans.

What do I mean by this? All pictures and videos you post using the app will automatically be deleted by the system after a period of time has already lapsed.

But how in the world did Snapchat manage to take such an odd feature and experience phenomenal growth, so that Facebook's big boss Mark Zuckerberg wanted to buy it for $3 billion? Further, what allowed it to grow so much to the point Zuckerberg's advances were turned away and instead, allowed Snapchat's parent company to go public via an initial public offering of its stocks?

What many people never realized, which the owners obviously did, was that there's a whole lot of people out there to whom such a temporary and passing nature of photos and videos appeal much. In fact, the owners probably realized far ahead of all of us that in general, we all interact and communicate with each other via moments that disappear afterwards. They created an app that – whether purposefully or not – mimics that way of human interaction, allowing it to click with millions and millions of people

Snapchat is a classic case of going contrarian when it came to niche marketing. Generally speaking, one of the key strengths of the Internet that a lot of people have come to love and value is the ability to create, document or save just about everything in digital form.

Chapter 1: The Single-Minded Secret To Growing Your Website Or Business

The genius of Snapchat is going the "wrong way" – if you will – on a seemingly one-way digital street by creating an app that automatically deletes uploaded pictures and videos after a predetermined amount of time. In fact, it kinda went back to the old days when TV first became popular in households, where you can only watch TV programs once and its gone forever.

So who was Snapchat's niche market in the beginning? Well, Facebook already covered the 25 year old and above market and Instagram (bought by Facebook) covered the 18-to-25 year old market, which left the Facebook conglomerate needing to fill in the gap of one other demographic: teenagers. And this was the niche that Snapchat saw as unserviced by the existing big social media platforms.

Snapchat seems to have correctly identified 2 important preferences or "needs" of teenagers today: not to be associated with their folks on social media and privacy. Even better is this: Snapchat seems to have effectively addressed these 2 preferences of today's teenagers with the automatic deletion feature of the app. How?

Initially, Facebook was the coolest thing since ice cream among the teenagers. But as the social media giant became even bigger, more and more parents – and even grandparents – started flocking in to the social media site. As such, many of today's teenagers started to become more and more disenfranchised by the ever-growing presence of "oldies" on social media, which was often times used to police or monitor them. As such, more and more teenagers started to look for a new social media place to stay – one where their parents won't be able to reach them on the web.

Enter Snapchat. Teenagers using Snapchat – particularly its auto-delete features – is the equivalent of them hanging "do not enter or knock" signs outside their rooms to keep their folks out and maintain their privacy. This feature hit the nail on teenagers' heads that just within a year of being formally launched, Snapchat's active followers already reached 10 million. Talk about growth hacking, eh?

Chapter 2:

Finding Your Niche – What The Market Wants

Now that you know the importance of focusing your efforts on a specific market niche, it's time to find out how to find the best market niche for your existing business – whose growth you want to accelerate – or planned business so you can maximize the result of your efforts. Fortunately, doing so isn't as complicated as rocket science.

Choosing A Profitable Niche

The first thing you'd need to do is to find out what is it you're passionate about or interested in. The reason for this is that you will have a higher chance of succeeding because you don't have to force yourself to learn about or research the subject or the topic. Not only would it be easier for you, it will also be a big boost in terms of confidence.

Another thing to consider when it comes to finding your niche are the things that you are naturally good at. Again, this minimizes the effort you need to exert when it comes to making a very good product or providing excellent service because you no longer have to master it or if there's anything that you still need to learn about it, it won't be much.

You can ask yourself what are the things that you can come up with or create. Choose things that you are naturally good at or are already knowledgeable of, which you can use as a good basis for choosing the right Market niche and coming up with a good product or service.

The next thing you will need to consider, which is the more important one, is whether or not the niche you're considering is something that is profitable and has high growth potential. In other words, is it a market Niche that has a big unmet need or preference that you can take advantage of? And if so, is the product or service your business provides or plans to provide something that enough people actually want and are willing to pay for?

Estimating Demand

One of the best things you can do to estimate market demand for a particular Niche or product, which won't cost you anything other than time and effort, is to make use of free keyword tools like Google AdWords.

By using such tools, you can estimate how popular a particular topic market niche is by studying the number of people who are researching about certain keywords and phrases that are related or pertaining to a particular topic or niche. When you do keyword research using such tools, you'll have a good estimate if the niche or product you are considering is one that many many people are very interested in.

When looking for a market Niche to focus on, it's very easy to prioritize those that have a very high volume of search traffic for certain related keywords or groups of keywords. However, I strongly advise that you avoid doing so because it means that particular Market Niche or topic it's one that has a lot of competition where in much bigger businesses spent a lot of marketing money.

That being said, it would be very hard for you to compete successfully especially if you're just a new business.

While this is not a rule of thumb, I highly recommend sticking to Market Niche results with keywords or groups of keywords registering no less than 5,000 monthly searches and no more than 30,000. Anything more than 30,000 may indicate a large amount of competition while anything less than 5,000 monthly searches is an indication very low or weak interest in that particular Market niche.

You would also have to consider the effects of seasonality when it comes to the average number of monthly searches on a particular niche or topic's keywords. Examples of niches or topics whose search volumes tend to be seasonal include Christmas gift ideas and delicious hot soup recipes, both of which are more popular during the holiday and winter seasons. Do consider the effect of seasonality because it may be that you choose a particular niche because at the time you did your Google AdWords research, it was peak season.

Doing so runs you the risk of choosing market Niche or topic that is not really popular. On the other hand, may be possible to reject a potentially profitable Market niche simply because it was off peak or off-season when you did your research.

Using The Google AdWords Keyword Tool

Before anything else, keep in mind that no tool can perfectly determine if a product or a niche will be a very marketable or profitable one. So if somebody tells you that the system they're marketing is able to do that, you are talking to a huckster – a scam artist. Run as far away and as fast as possible if you want to keep your hard earned money and spend it on what's truly legit and good.

That being said, using tools like the Google AdWords Keyword Tool can significantly raise the chances of you being able to choose the ideal or best niche for your current or planned business to focus its marketing efforts on.

One way to check if your niche will most likely be a profitable one or one that has enough market demand is through the number of ads on the platform that specific keywords or phrases have. When companies put out ads, they do so with the expectation of being able to generate substantial amounts of sales for their products or services.

In particular, advertisers will run ads based on certain keywords or phrases.

If you want to see how these AdWords ads look like, do a search on Google for a keyword like "holistic health practices" for example. Check out the results page. On top of the results page – usually the first several results – are the ads related to that keyword.

You will know that they are paid ads because right below the heading on the leftmost side, you will see a box that says "Ad". If for some reason, you don't see any such ads on top of first page of search results for a specific keyword, it means no one cares to run ads for that keyword or phrase because no one thinks it's worth paying ads for, i.e., demand is not enough for it to be a profitable keyword.

Now if you see that for all the major keywords or phrases you searched for don't have ads, then it's a clear sign that the niches for which you're considering those keywords don't have enough market demand to be profitable.

If the keyword searches yield ads at the top of the first search results page, then the next logical step is to estimate how much money advertisers are willing to pay to have their ads for those keywords posted on top of the first page of search results for those keywords.

The more money advertisers are willing to pay, the higher the interest or possible demand is for such keywords and consequently, the niches in which those keywords are used. In other words, it's a good indicator of potential high profitability.

Average Cost-Per-Click (CPC)

CPC refers to how much advertisers are willing to pay for the ads they want to put out on Google. The higher the average CPC bids, the higher the perceived profitability for certain keywords. You can check out the average CPC for specific keywords related to the niche you're interested in using the Google AdWords Keyword Tool.

So what is CPC or cost per click? This gives you an idea of how much advertisers pay on average every time people click on the ads they posted on Google's search page. If people are curious to know more about specific ads, they will click on it and will be directed to a landing webpage of the advertiser's choice.

If the percentage of people who click on those keyword ads convert into paying customers, it means there's good demand for the niches associated with the keyword and as such, are deemed to be a profitable ones. The higher the profitability of certain keywords are, the higher the average CPC bid of advertisers.

Basically, just go through your list of keywords related to the niches your considering and check out the results of their CPCs. In particular, you should be focusing your attention on keywords or niches with high average CPCs and low competition, i.e., less than 10 ads competing for it.

But even if it's not exactly that, you can still consider niches where people are generally spending money on and those that you feel can still give you a good return for your money.

Shortlisting Your Niche

If after considering the keywords related to your niche or topic, you find that there's less than 5,000 monthly searches individually or even combined, it's may be indicative of lack of market demand. It means that if you still pursue that niche, there's a high probability your business won't be profitable or grow significantly enough over time.

You'd be better off looking for another niche that has higher search results by going broader or more general with the topic. For example, if the niche on "holistic eye health" yields minimal search results monthly, go higher with "holistic health practices" instead, which may yield a high enough search results.

If on the other hand, your niche's keywords yield to high results, i.e., too competitive with more than 30,000 searches monthly, then you'd be better off by going deeper or more specific. Using the earlier example, if the search results for "holistic health practices" seem too high and competitive, try narrowing the niche down to "holistic eye health practices" or "holistic oral health practices".

Keep in mind that this process is usually done several times and it's hardly ever the case that you find the ideal niche in just one go. Patience and perseverance will be your ally in finding the right niche for your business and growth hacking it.

Social Media

When it comes to expressing one's self, social media is the undisputed venue. As such, it can be a great place to check out people's general sentiments, ideas, and interests. While social media sites are generally diluted with too much personal expressions, knowing exactly where to look can give you much insights as to the markets' underlying preferences. In short, it's another good way to find a niche to focus on.

Let's take a look at some of the most obvious social media places to go for market insights. One is of course Facebook. Most – if not all brands – are already on Facebook and their respective pages on the social media site are where they tend to interact with their customers or would be customers.

Of particular use are the comments sections, where people can express their sentiments, suggestions, or desire for something in particular. This can prove to be quite a treasure chest of insights as to what could potentially be a profitable niche with lots of potential for growth.

Twitter's another place to check out, particularly the trending hashtags. By checking out these trending hashtags, you can get a good idea of what's popular as of the moment and a potential trail back to what can be a very profitable market niche.

Forums

Outside of social media sites, online forums are another great place to check out for insights concerning potentially profitable and high-growth niches. Often times, its people who are serious about a certain topic or issue that create or participate in most online forums.

Online forums such as Reddit and Quora are excellent places to mine for information on what people are looking for and consequently, potentially profitable niches. Websites like these offer so many discussion boards on a wide range of topics. And in these discussion boards, you can find lots of people expressing their unmet needs and even suggestions for potential solutions that you can take to the next level.

The key to maximizing these online forums is being able to spot recurring themes or ideas. Not because many people expressed their preference or desire for something once or twice doesn't mean it's already a profitable niche to focus on.

But if you find that it keeps on repeating over a period of time, then you may have a goldmine of a niche in your hands. Or even if it's not something that's often repeated but if you see that meeting such a need or preference can be a gateway to being the first to corner a potentially profitable niche, then by all means consider it.

One type of forum that can give you lots of insights are product forums, also referred to as support forums. In particular, support forums of products and services related to your existing business (competitors) or a business or industry you're planning to get into.

Chapter 3:

Visibility – The Gateway To Growth Hacking

The key to growth is increasing the demand for your business' products and services. But even if you choose the best keywords and the ideal market niche to focus in order to give your business that exceptional growth you desire, it's not gonna fly if people don't know your business exists. In other words, you can't hack growth without being visible to many people first.

And in this chapter, we'll take a look at ways you can optimize your business' visibility so that you can increase its chances of growing significantly.

SEO

And we're back to discussing keywords. Only this time, we won't use them for finding niches but to improve your business' online visibility. Times have indeed changed and at this point in time, Google – the search engine of all search engines – has evolved much to the point that in many instances, it knows what end users really need. This makes using the right keywords for your business' online content very, very important for SEO.

Speaking of which, SEO refers to search engine optimization, a process whose goal is to rank a particular webpage as high as possible when ever certain keywords are searched on Google or other search engines.

For example, if your business is providing bookkeeping services to small businesses, SEO is the process of making sure your business' web page or social media page will rank as high as possible whenever searches for the keywords "small business bookkeeping services" or "small business accounting services" are ran on Google and other search engines. Obviously, the higher the ranking, the higher the online visibility.

While SEO can be quite a lengthy and complicated topic to cover in this book, there are some practical ways you can optimize your business' website's search engine ranking. The first one is to identify those key phrases or words that potential customers would most likely use when looking up on search engines.

Another practical SEO step you can take is that when you find such keywords, make sure that they're included in your online contents' title pages, descriptions, main text body, and the like. To be even more efficient, consider using different keywords for different areas of your business' website or social media posts.

Through The Backdoor

Another way to improve visibility is through what are called "backlinks". These are links featured on websites that when clicked on, lead you to another website. While that may sound so simple, it actually is, it isn't as easy as you think it may be. Don't worry though, it isn't rocket science and with enough guidance, you can use backlinking to improve your business' or startups online visibility for successful growth hacking. Here are some of the best ways to do it.

Blogs

One important aspect of inbound marketing – or drawing people in as a form of marketing instead of going after them – is through blogs. These are great avenues to showcase your business in ways that aren't as "market-y" as advertisements and banners.

Even better, you get a chance to show your target niche the personal side of your business, which includes you and your expertise. If people see you – the owner - as one that can be trusted both in terms of character and capabilities, the higher your chances of converting them into paying and loyal customers.

More than just showcasing you and your company, maintaining a blog site also helps your business' visibility by potentially increasing your rankings in search results for certain keywords. In particular, your chances of climbing up the search engine results ladder go up as you add more pages on your blog site.

When it comes to coming up with regular content on your business' blog or website, you don't have to come up with something unique each and every time. Even if you wanted to, it's just not feasible as you'll quickly run out of unique ideas to post.

Instead, consider regenerating or rewriting previously published materials by adding your personal touch to it, i.e., additional facts, examples, or thoughts. And when the ideas are unique to a specific author, cite that author and always re-write content – never publish verbatim. If you do, you'll be charged with plagiarism, which will get you into a whole lot of legal and marketing trouble.

And when it comes to blogging, don't limit yourself to your or your business' blog site only. Another way you can maximize the power of blogs is by guest blogging, or writing blog entries on other people's or business' blogs! In fact, I believe that's a better way of increasing visibility than your own blog site because it effectively increases your audience immediately. Why? When you guest blog, you expose yourself or your business to other people's or business' audiences.

And because the blogger allowed you to write a guest post, that's an implicit way of telling his or her own audience that "Hey, this blogger over here is someone I approve of. You can trust him or her!"

PR Networks

When it comes to public relations, you don't have to spend a fortune as many top companies do. On the Internet, there are a couple of online portals where you can get free PR, and one of those is Help A Reporter Out or HARO. This portal allows authors, bloggers, and reporters to interact online and is a great way to get your business backlinked on other authors' or reporters' blog sites.

Here's how it works. Many authors and reporters, in the process of churning out published works, post questions on portals or sites like HARO. If you know the answers to their queries, you can take the opportunity to help them out by posting correct answers to their queries. In return for your favor, they'll give you a backlink in their published works, which can help promote your business to a much wider audience that you couldn't have otherwise reached.

Product Reviews

You can ask popular bloggers in your niche to do a product or service review of your business on their blog sites, which will of course include a backlink to your business. It can be a win-win situation for the both of you as bloggers are constantly on the lookout for great ideas for engaging content and you're looking for increased exposure to new audiences within your target niche.

It may even entice other bloggers of the same niche to ask for the opportunity to try out your service or product for purposes of conducting their own reviews on their blog sites when they see a good product review of your business.

There are 2 things you'll need to get right for this to work, though. First is you have to make sure your product or service for review is of excellent quality. Mind you, I said excellent, not perfect. What good would a review be if the reviewer would most likely give a negative one. So make sure that the bloggers who'd review your business' product or service won't have legitimate reasons not to write good reviews.

The other thing you'll need to get right is choosing the right bloggers to review your product or service. Otherwise, you'll just be wasting time, effort, and maybe even money. Obviously, you'd want to go for the most respected bloggers in the niche you're targeting and when I say most respected, I mean they have both a large following and a good reputation.

Niche Forums And Sites

Websites and forums that are highly targeted on specific demographic groups or niches are another goldmine for great backlinks. You can submit your business' website or online store to any such forums or websites as many of these places are on the look out for new products and services to feature as a way of consistently generating engaging content. As they feature yours, a backlink is expected, which will direct readers to your business' online store or website, as the case may be.

Writing Comments

Earlier, I talked about mining the comments sections of online articles, blogs, and social media posts for ideas on what people are looking for or want. However, you can look at the comments section in a whole new different way for boosting your business' online visibility – you'll be the one writing comments this time.

Why would you want to do this? It's because doing so improves online visibility in 2 ways: SEO and backlinks. Let's talk about backlinks first.

You can provide your very own backlinks on other people's or business' blogs, online articles, and social media posts through the comments section. It's that easy. Here's the better part – if more and more websites backlink to your business, search engines will have a higher chance of thinking that your business' website has enough quality content for certain keywords in your target niche.

You get enough visibility from people who read the comments section of the websites you comment on and improve your search engine results at the same time. Talk about hitting two birds with one stone, eh?

While it can be very easy to do that, doing it right isn't. It's because not all website owners are keen on backlinking on their comments section because for them, it smells like spamming. That's why you need to use this technique with caution.

Ensure that when you post a backlink to your business' website, make sure that it's very much within context of the discussion thread of the posted article, blog entry, or social media post. So if the thread is discussing the merits and demerits of Donald Trump's travel ban, don't post a back link in the comments section, especially if your business is a lingerie store.

Chapter 4:

Engagement – The Secret To Growth Hacking

Alright. Let's assume for a moment that you already know which niche to target and have successfully drawn enough web traffic to your business website, blog, or social media page. That my friend isn't the end of the growth hacking journey.

It's because they haven't done anything yet to contribute to your business' growth – they haven't taken any favorable action.

In this chapter, we'll talk about the secret sauce to enjoying substantial growth in your business – engagement. And when we say engagement, we mean the process of grabbing and keeping audiences' attention and more importantly, make them respond favorably.

The content on your business' webpage or on the ads that you put out must be able to grab and keep your target audiences' attention and convince them to take the right action. The engagement process is nowhere near about you – it's about your target audience.

In other words, the content your business will put out on cyberspace must consider what your audience is interested in, what they want, and how they understand things. Not about what you're interested in, what you want, and how you understand things.

When you're able to engage your target audience or niche with quality content, you're able to connect with them on an emotional level. And in order for you to create engaging content, you must learn the characteristics that make up such.

Strong Headlines

It's no different from the old days of printed publications. Magazines and newspapers with strong headlines scream the loudest and get the most attention from curious passersby and as such, tend to sell more copies than those with weak headlines. It's no different when it comes to your business' online content – strong headlines can effectively engage your target audience to the point that they take the first beneficial action for your business: read the rest of the content.

According to statistics from the website www.copyblogger.com, about 80% of people will read your contents' headlines but of that percentage, only 20% will continue reading the rest of the content.

To make strong headlines, don't rush for the sake of coming up with one. Take your time and come up with several headlines for each of your content or posts so you can have a point of comparison.

Don't settle – if none among the lineup catches your fancy, brainstorm again to come up with more. Remember, your headlines are the point of first contact and if your content doesn't get traction with your target audience at the onset, it won't get any traction at all.

Action Instruction

Ok, it should've read call to action but hey, I like rhymes. But seriously speaking, another characteristic or element of an engaging piece of content is the ability to be applied practically. In other words, engaging content in most cases, is content that's actionable.

There are 2 ways that a particular piece of content is actionable. First is application. This is particularly true for content that seeks to help people solve problems, address issues, or simply make their lives much better.

Engaging content is one where after reading, the audience knows exactly what to do in terms of applying what they learned to specific issues they're facing or goals they set for themselves. A sign of an un-engaging piece of content is the question "what do I do next" after reading it.

In order for your instructional or informational content to be actionable in the sense that it can be practically applied, you can give specific examples of how that's done – or has been done already in the past – or specific instructions on how to do so. You can even give both for higher actionability!

This is one type of calls to action, or appeals for your audience to act favorably on your content.

And when it comes to actionable content in terms of application, it's important the content isn't degrading or condescending to the readers. Some people write informational or instructional content that sounds as if they're talking down on their audience and making them feel like they're stupid or something.

Even if your content is very practical and actionable, it won't gain traction with your audience and keep you from hacking growth simply by turning people off. They won't care about what you know, which is shared in the content of your posts or blog entries, when they know you don't care about them.

The second way a piece of content, whether online or off, is actionable is if it's clear what you want the audience to do with the content. The content you post won't always be instructional or informational, just like TV commercials or print ads.

For such content, you will need to persuade the audience to act in your favor, e.g., liking, commenting, or sharing the content.

While it's nice and all to know that the content you put out for marketing your business touches people's lives, the only way it can help your business experience phenomenal growth is via action. When people like or comment on your posts, it means that your content was able to connect with them personally.

And when people see that many people approve of your business' online content via likes and favorable comments, it helps persuade them that it's worth reading or watching to the end as well as adding social proof to your content. But even better is people sharing your content, which is the primary determinant of whether or not your content will become viral, which we'll discuss in the next chapter.

But suffice to say, phenomenal growth in your business or startup will only happen when many enough people see your business as fast as possible. And the key to rapid promotion of your business – for free – is via your audience's cooperation via sharing.

As with the first type of actionable content, it's important to include instructions of how you would like to your audience to proceed after reading or watching your content. Example of these are "Like us on Facebook", "Click on the button below to subscribe", and "Click "like" and share", among others. This is another kind of call to action.

Calls to action are important because in many instances, audiences need to be instructed on what to do next after they've viewed your content. You can't blame them as they probably have many other things on their minds.

If they like your content enough, calls to action is that one soft nudge that propels them to act favorably on your content, which will promote your business even more (for free) and bring them steps closer to possibly becoming your paying customers.

Give Answers

If I ask you why did God create Google and other search engines, you'd probably answer, "to find the answers to life's questions, both major and minor!" If you did, you get an "A" for A-ffort!

Kidding aside, you'd be correct to assume that – search engines were created to help people get answers to their most perplexing questions as fast and as convenient as possible.

When it comes to reading blog and article posts on your business' website, blog site, or social media page, it's highly possible that they're looking to answer a particular question in their minds or a specific need they have at the moment, whether it's the need to satisfy a particularly nagging curiosity about cross-stitching or being unable to sleep at night until they figured out the answer to "what is the square root of 10,439.45?"

The need to be entertained with a hearty laugh or a particularly riveting piece of fictional content are reasons why people may want to read your business' content.

And the ability of your content to satisfactorily meet those needs or wants, i.e., answer their curiosity and satiate their hunger for information be it recreational or practical, and align the answers to your business' products or services will help your business experience potentially phenomenal growth.

Reliable

I want you to ponder on this before reading further: have you ever read an article, blog, or social media post that turned out to be inaccurate to say the least and at worst, totally false? I have and I'm telling you I didn't just delete those websites, blogs, and social media pages from my list of favorites, I also made sure to tell the people in my social media circles to avoid them.

They didn't just lose an existing member of their audiences, they lost potential ones as well. Talk about double whammy.

Now put yourself on those erroneous – or maliciously inaccurate – blog sites, websites, and social media pages. How do you think that's affected your business in general and your growth hacking endeavors in particular? You see the picture? That's why when you put out content online in order to promote your business, you have to be very careful that what you're posting is accurate.

If your posts and comments are generally wrong or inaccurate, it will reflect on your business as one that may not be trustworthy. Without trust, your business won't just stagnate – it'll die!

To help your content – and consequently, you and your business – become more reliable, consider the possibility of including links to other sites, which can help bolster your integrity. How? By showing that it's not just you who believes in the stuff you put in your content and that the facts and figures you put there come from reliable sources.

That being said, you must pay careful attention to who or where you're linking to, i.e., they must be sources with high integrity and authority. The more quality links you provide, the more trust you can build for your business with your audience.

Linking isn't just helpful for establishing reliability. It's also helpful in terms of online visibility. When you link your content to other content and sites, it allows search engines to get a better idea of what your content or site's about and to better categorize it. Therefore, you can hit 2 birds with one stone with linking.

Provoking

No, I'm not talking about picking a fight with your audience. What I mean by this is your content needs to pique the interest and curiosity of the people who'll come across it. With being provoked, your audience won't act accordingly on the content you post.

One way to provoke your audience is to write an urgent and promising introduction to the content. How's this helpful? It grabs their attention from the get go, which will start the ball rolling in terms of reading or watching the rest of your content.

We live in a day and age where people are bombarded with so much information on a daily basis and as such, they tend to make very quick judgments as to which things are worthy of their very limited time and attention.

With an urgent and promising intro, your content's chances of being able to cut through the sea of information your audiences swim in and stand out so that they'll be convinced to give it the chance to be fully read or watched.

If at first your content doesn't succeed, there's no more opportunity for it to try again so it has to grab the audiences' attention at the onset.

Once you're able to grab their attention, another way to provoke their minds and hearts is by using stories to illustrate the points your trying to make. Why? People in general love stories, period.

But more than that, stories can help make relatively complicated information much more relatable and therefore, understandable. And that makes for great engagement.

Lastly, you can provoke your audience and engage them well by ending your content with a question or questions. These are meant to stir the interest or curiosity of the audience regarding your content. Also, there's a belief that information that's immediately acted on is information that's processed well and remembered over the long term.

By asking questions that are meant to be answered by your audience, you engage them by making them act on the information you just gave, i.e., reflect on its applicability in their lives.

To the extent that you're able to positively provoke your audience with your content is the extent to which it can get a lot of comments. The advantage of garnering lots of comments is visibility – better SEO for your content. Being up-to-date is one of the important areas search engines evaluate content in terms of ranking for searches for certain keywords.

With many comments, it tells search engines that your content is updated regularly.

Add Visuals

Ever wondered why people say that pictures paint thousands of words? Well it's because of the fact that we all think in pictures. When you ask memory masters such as Kevin Trudeau how they're able to memorize many things very quickly and effectively, they'll tell you that one of the secrets is visualization – associating that which you're trying to memorize with strong images.

In this regard, you can make your content more engaging by using videos, pictures, tables, or graphs instead of purely words. When people literally get a good picture of what you're trying to say, they'll respond to it much better and the chances of them acting favorably on your content is much higher compared to not using visuals.

Just a word of caution – only use visuals that are highly relevant and will be able to clearly get your point across. Otherwise, don't bother using visuals as they will just become distractions to what your content is really trying to say.

Short And Sweet

Lastly, it's important to remember that for most people, time is a luxury. With so many things to do, they're looking for ways to get the most bang for their time bucks and no matter how informative and entertaining your content is, they won't hang out long enough to finish reading or watching it. In fact, if they see at the onset that it's long, they'd ditch it without giving it a chance.

Another thing that will help make your content more engaging is using bullets to segregate your contents main ideas. Bullet points allow readers to quickly get an overview of what the content is about and make judgments as to whether or not it'll be worth their time.

Using bullets also makes the idea or ideas in your content more organized, which helps your audience understand them clearly. Think of how you scan through a book that you're thinking about buying. Normally, you scan through the table of contents to get a general idea of what it's really about. The table of contents is just a long form bullet point presentation of the books content.

You can do a substantially shorter or more concise version for your online content.

Chapter 5:

Taking It Higher – Going Viral

Do you remember that phenomenal song Gangnam Style by the Korean music sensation Psy? Remember how it broke the back of YouTube figuratively by being the first video to garner over a billion views...and counting.

If you're looking for the best picture of content going viral, that would be it. People liking, sharing, and viewing it over and over again – can't get enough of the stuff during the time it was smoldering hot like steel in a furnace.

In essence, viral content is engaging content on steroids. While going viral isn't a pre-requisite for your startup's long-term growth and success, it's the secret to phenomenal growth that can propel your start up or existing business to the next levels of success at the shortest possible time. In other words, it's the fast track to growth hacking.

And here are several ways to help increase your contents' chances of going viral. They may not allow your business' videos to achieve over 1 billion views but they can help it more popular with more and more people and increase your chances of successfully hacking growth for your business.

Celebrity And News References

Whether or not you're into the Kardashians, you know that referencing your content to that family – especially if the reference is huge, i.e., getting them to retweet or share your content – can do wonders to help make your content go viral. Or if you can get Stephen Curry to share a link to your business' website, you know that going viral is just a matter of time, or hours. It's because celebrities already have a huge following and that makes it easy to leverage for going viral.

A friend of mine leverages the status of celebrities by giving sample of the cool stuff she sells online to a couple of celebrities, in the hope that they enjoy them and post on their social media that they use such stuff and make reference to my friend.

She was able to go viral – at least on a minor scale – when a relatively famous person she sent a sample of the smartphone cases to, posted about it on Instagram. It's safe to say that she laughed herself all the way to the bank for that month as her online store became viral due to that celebrity's post.

Another reference that can pay viral dividends for your content is to tie the content to unfolding news stories or current events.

Why? They're already viral to begin with and tying up to a viral piece of content is akin to cuddling up with a person that has the flu – there's a high probability of getting the virus itself. Only in this case, it's the virality and not a virus you'll be hoping to catch.

I did this several times with posts on Facebook. I'd write a blog-like post about a topic and link it to an ongoing major piece of NBA news and often times, it reaches thousands of people more compared to my posts with no current events or news references or links. It was like standing on the shoulders of giants.

Just be careful to link with news or events that are highly relevant to the content at hand. Otherwise, it may not work.

Myth Busting

Ever wondered how the show Myth Busters aired on the National Geographic channel was able to garner such a huge cult following? It's because of the subject of the show itself – myths! Content that aims to provide information by busting popular myths is therefore a great way to attract much attention and gain a somewhat viral status.

For example, your business is into providing accounting software to small businesses. You can put out content about "The 5 Most Common Myths About Why Accounting Software Isn't For Your Small Business" or "The 3 Biggest Myths About Why Accountants Don't Want You To Use Accounting Software".

Just make sure that the myth that's related to your business' products or services that you'll solve in order to promote your business is one that's familiar with many people. Otherwise, it may not be of great help.

Common Mistakes

As with myth busting, people are very much interested how to avoid making mistakes – especially very serious ones. This is because according to success Guru Tony Robbins, there are only 2 major motivations for us doing what we're doing: love of pleasure and fear of pain. Content that dwells on how to sidestep major mistakes appeals to the second motivation of pain avoidance.

And it would be much, much better if your content is able to subtly introduce your business' products and services as one of the ways to avoid or sidestep the major mistakes identified in the content.

Challenge The Status Quo

Another way to increase your chances of making your content – and consequently your business – go viral is by referencing it to a widely held belief and challenging it. It brings provocation to a whole new level and as a result, bring the intensity and amount of engagement your business gets to a higher level as well.

Just make sure that as you challenge a widely held belief or status quo, you don't do it disrespectfully or condescendingly. Do so in a confident yet respectful way that will earn the respect and approval of even the staunchest opposition.

Use Numbered Lists

For some strange reason, using a numbered list helps make information much more interesting and appealing. Posts or articles entitled "10 Ways To Make Her Fall In Love With You" is definitely more appealing than "How To Make Her Fall In Love With You" because you get a much clearer idea of what to expect in the article.

Comparisons

Another particular area of great interest for most people are rivalries or competitions. As such, incorporating comparisons into your content will help make it more viral-worthy. If you're providing accounting services for example, a potentially viral-worthy post that can help promote your business to much wider audiences is "Why Hiring An Accountant Can Be More Profitable For Your Business Than DIY Accounting".

With comparisons, the benefits or costs can be highlighted even more and make more and more people interested in the content and possibly, make the content and your business go viral.

Chapter 6:

Keeping Them Glued

The last piece of the growth hacking puzzle is to ensure you retain the audience you've already garnered through highly engaging content that's targeted at the right niche for your business. Your business' ability to grow is dependent on your ability to sustain the interest or following of its audiences long enough to become satisfied paying customers.

When you're able to keep 'em glued to your business' it means you've done a good job of servicing their needs and wants. That increases the likelihood of them telling other people about your business, which can continue expanding your market and eventually, paying customers.

In this chapter, we'll take a look at how you can increase your odds of successfully retaining your captured audience en route to converting them into loyal paying customers that'll propel your startup or existing business to new heights of growth.

Keep It Personal

Whether you believe it or not, business is all about relationships. The extent you're able to establish good relationships with your customers and potential customers is the extent to which you can get their business and continue doing business with them. And guess what – relationships personal.

Now, I'm not saying you treat your customers like the way you treat your best buds, i.e., slapping them hard on the butt, hugging them like there's no tomorrow, or busting their balls for a good laugh. No, that's not the kind of personal I'm talking about.

I'm talking about giving your business' audience a relatively personalized experience of the business, especially online. For example, you can create customized landing web pages. A good example of this is the Amazon Store, particularly the Kindle Store.

Whenever I go the Kindle Store to browse for books, they've already arranged a lineup of recommended books based on those I already purchased or downloaded samples of. That really makes life much easier for me when it comes to satiating my appetite for continuous reading and it makes earning money off me easier for them too. It's a win-win situation!

Now I'm not saying you'll have to be as highly technical as Amazon. What I'm saying is be creative enough to give your audiences as much of a personalized experience as possible.

It might be in the form of different segments or versions of the same product or service based on a particular need or preference, or allowing them to post questions or comments on your business' social media or web pages.

Ensure Accessibility

Another way to make sure you keep your captured audience is ensuring that your business is reachable anytime and anywhere. And the best way to do this is maintaining an active online presence where they can email, message or get in touch with you and on 2 platforms: computer and mobile devices such as smartphones or tablets.

Considering that more and more people are using smartphones more than their computers when it comes to social media and other online activities, creating an app for your business can be a very great way of attracting and keeping audiences glued to you and your business.

Always Be Relevant

Nothing else can bore the hell out of your already captured audience than always seeing the same old content for weeks on end on your business' social media, blog, or web pages. Considering the massive amounts of information people are exposed to on a daily basis these days, consider it a great privilege – one that must be defended at all reasonable costs – to have earned and to maintain.

When you're able to keep your business' web, blog, and social media pages current and updated with relevant content, you'll be able to ensure constant engagement and potentially, continuously repeating business and endorsements – two of the most important things when it comes to your business' growth hacking efforts.

Also, make sure that when you post new content, it's highlighted. That'll ensure that your audience sees them as soon as possible. It'll also do you good to create a page or section where you can collectively feature the most popular contents you find from other sources that are related to your business.

Chapter 6: Keeping Them Glued

It'll be easier for you audience to access great and updated content as well as get the impression that your business is well connected and sufficiently diverse.

Send Regular Emails

Sending your audience or followers regular emails or messages is a great way to stay in touch and keep engaged. The advantage of sending them emails or private messages regularly is you get to update them on what's happening to your business or the industry its in, which can help foster a deep sense of relationship with you and your business.

It also helps separate your business from the others by virtue of such a relatively personal relationship and by making it easier for them to get updated.

How can you get their emails or contact details? Offer a really cool freebie in return of their email address or other contact info. Some of the most common freebies are e-books or reports about a popular topic within your target niche. When you get their contact details, send them emails once a week.

I believe anything more frequent than that runs the risk of overwhelming your audience and make them ignore you and anything less frequent runs you and your business the risk of becoming irrelevant and uninteresting.

Reward Them

Finally, people in general are motivated to continue doing something for as long as they're rewarded for it. As such, you should reward your audiences, especially those who are already your loyal paying customers, in order to maintain their interest in and loyalty to your business.

Rewards don't need to be expensive – they don't need to cost at all! If you can write short e-books that are interesting and that contain information that isn't available elsewhere, you can give them free e-books every month. Or you can hire a ghostwriter on jobsites like UpWork.com, Freelancer.com, or Fiverr.com to do it for you for a reasonable price.

Chapter 7:

Growth Hacking – Keeping It Practical

As we end this book, I'd like to discuss a very important component of growth hacking that many people tend to overlook: budgeting. It's very easy to lose sight of the primary reason for wanting to grow the business in terms of number of customers and amount of sales, which is higher net profits, and end up with less income or worse, net losses.

Yes, you should do as much as you possibly can to make sure you identify the right niche to target, making your target audiences find you on the Web, and use engaging content to win them over and keep them. And the demarcation line that objectively tells you when enough is enough is an established budget.

Don't embark on a growth hacking mission without first knowing how much money you can spend for the mission. Otherwise, it can be fairly easy to lose a lot of money and defeat the purpose for which you embarked on growth hacking.

When you've established your total budget, identify the different tactics you'll need to employ to hack your business' growth. Divide your budget accordingly among those tactics so that each tactic has a budgetary limit to keep your finances in check and ensure that you spend more on what's most important and spend less on those that aren't as important.

If you're working with a team on your business' growth hacking initiative, make sure that the total and sub-budgets are clear to all members of the team, especially to the people who are responsible for a particular tactic.

Make them accountable for the amounts they spend so that they'll be conscious about spending money responsibly and not just blow through the budgets given them.

Best Things In Life Are (Sometimes) Free

While it's true that the most of the companies or entrepreneurs that were able to successfully grow their startups or small businesses spent fortunes to do so, you don't have to necessarily follow the paths they took and blow much money away. With the right strategies and tactics, you can make use of free tools to grow your company.

Using Google AdWords and scouring through Facebook pages, blogs, forums, and other niche sites for useful information as to what the market wants – and therefore point you to the right direction – are free.

It just takes more work though. But then again, your money at this point in your business' life and size must be spent on those that are critical for its continued operations and as such, the extra work will be well worth it.

Guest blogging, doing simple SEO by yourself or asking an expert friend to do it pro bono, and backlinking are relatively cheap or free ways to improve your business' online visibility.

Again, it may entail a bit more work but it's still going to be worth it.

And lastly, keeping your audiences locked and glued in on your business via regular and engaging content is something you can do yourself. With enough patience and wisdom, you can generate such content that will help your business experience massive growth in the soonest possible time.

Keep Your Eye On The Prize

Finally, never let your eyes veer away from profitability. Even if you manage to stay well within your growth hacking budget, you can still experience losses if you don't watch your business overall expenses. Consider the cost of producing its products or rendering the services it offers – can you bring it down further?

There are instances that growth hacking can occur even with little or no increase in the number of customers or the amount of sales. By slashing costs significantly while maintaining or even enhancing the quality of products and services, many businesses have been able to experience phenomenal growth in income.

Conclusion

Growth hacking is neither rocket science nor some sort of mystical practice that is exclusive to those who possess esoteric knowledge. It's something that all entrepreneurs can do using practical and effective courses of action such as those you learned in this book.

But in order for you to start hacking your business' growth, one more thing is needed - something that's only available from you and from no one and nowhere else.

Action!

Knowing is just half the battle and the other half is applying what you know. That's why I strongly recommend – no, I am compelling you – to apply what you learned from this book as soon as possible. You don't have to do everything in one fell swoop. You just need to take the first small step, then the next, and then the next – until you completely apply all you've learned here.

Another good way to act on what you learned here is by digging deeper into the techniques outlined in this book. Either way, don't let one week pass without doing anything about what you read here. If you don't, may be missing out on one of the greatest opportunities of our generation!

Chapter 7: Growth Hacking – Keeping It Practical

Lastly if you enjoyed this book, it would be much appreciated if you could leave a review on Amazon. The best way for this book to make its way into the hands of more readers is through truthful reviews about this work. Please write what you liked about this book and what could be improved upon. Any and all feedback is helpful as I continue to serve the needs of my readership.

Here's to your success my friend, Cheers!